MODERN BUSINESS ETIQUETTE

MODERN BUSINESS ETIQUETTE

What is expected of you professionally

Audrey Bonvin-Dechoux & Annabelle Utelli

ISBN-10: 1507819080

ISBN-13: 9781507819081

Library of Congress Control Number: 2015906956

CreateSpace Independent Publishing Platform
North Charleston, South Carolina

Contents

Introduction

How important is good etiquette in business?

You might have succeeded in your professional life, and you might feel that neither this question nor its answer concerns you. After all, you have made it so far, and you will keep on being successful. Or so you think. But in today's world, where competition is fiercer, lots of people are lining up to take your place or to impress your customers. Your competitors are not only those found on your street or in your town but those miles away from you.

So what do you do about it? How do you become a savvy professional?

We all have our own notions of business etiquette. Some avoid considering its importance because they fear or reject the rules and codes established by our predecessors. A lot of companies overlook the importance of business etiquette. They often believe that these skills are easy to master and unimportant to linger upon.

Business and social etiquettes are simply courteous codes of conduct, useful in communications and interactions in the business and social worlds. The purpose of these codes of conduct is for people to show mutual respect for one another. Etiquette facilitates encounters. Mastering business etiquette will make your meetings more harmonious and your image more professional.

With the evolution and globalization of etiquette, some codes of conduct have naturally been modified to facilitate contacts and communication. The fast-paced growth of technology keeps people constantly informed. However, the basic rules about conveying respect remain.

Being more aware of business etiquette will help you to feel at ease in all circumstances. It will give you a natural elegance and self-confidence. It will contribute to your success and reputation. On the other hand, the lack of business etiquette can ruin your credibility and tarnish your career or your business reputation.

After giving courses to people coming from different cultures and working in different fields and countries, we decided to write this book to share our experience and knowledge. The positive feedback we got from our clients and colleagues over the years made us realize how much our passion for business etiquette could help others.

In this book, we tried to illustrate the different chapters by sharing with you some of our personal life experiences.

Our professional background in luxury, hospitality, personal placement, and education gives us enough confidence to share our knowledge. We hope that our advices will be helpful for your coming life experiences.

Enjoy reading and learning.

Greeting People

What is the base of good communication?

Greeting someone properly is a sign of respect. It shows your consideration for the other person. Everybody likes to be taken into consideration and not feel ignored.

You are taught at a very young age to greet by saying *good morning, good afternoon,* etc. A person walking into your office or passing you in the corridor who does not greet you may come across as impolite and unprofessional.

In an institution where I was working, my colleagues expressed their frustration about a coworker who very often passed by without greeting people, at times even ignoring others. They thought she was rude and that she needed to learn manners. She was not a person the colleagues looked forward to having in a meeting. Her reputation as the unfriendly and cold colleague stayed with her throughout her time at that institution.

Greeting someone who walks into your company will take just a few seconds: "Good morning/Good afternoon/Good evening, Mr./Mrs./Miss Lucas," or "Good morning/Good afternoon/Good evening, Madam/Miss/Sir" (if you do not know his or her name). To this few-second speech, add a smile and make eye contact with the person you are addressing. This is already a good base to start a conversation.

Hi, hello, and *hey* should be reserved for people you are really acquainted with.

Do not take the liberty of shortening the name of your business partner or giving him or her a nickname. *Michael* is not *Mickey* because it suits you or because you find it funny. By using a nickname, you might seem friendly but not too credible or professional.

SHAKING HANDS

What does your handshake say about you?

I had broken my knee and gotten an operation. One Sunday, I felt pain and had to go back in, an emergency. After I'd waited awhile with pain and frustration, a young doctor finally came in. Her handshake was a soft, lifeless handshake. That surprised me in a negative way; I had trouble trusting her.

Unconsciously, we make opinions of people depending on their handshakes. Some will tell you that you cannot change your handshake as it is personal, linked to you. Your handshake is personal, but you can work on having a good grip that inspires confidence. I have worked on mine over the years.

There are, of course, different types of handshakes, which leave different opinions or impressions:

- Horizontal handshake: The most common handshake, this one indicates that this person considers you at his or her same level—no inferiority or superiority.

- High (chest-level) handshake: Often seen in social environments, this shake tends to be reserved for people who like taking care of others.
- Low (below-the-belt) handshake: This shake is common among those who intend to lead. Twisting the grip to be on top is also another sign of leadership.

Which handshake do you use?

How do you react to the different handshakes?

- If someone grabs your hand too hard (bone crushing), you can try to pull off slowly or open your palm to indicate that you are letting go. The person will release the grip, unless he or she is doing it on purpose.
- If the person places his or her palm in your hand without taking hold, do not take it personally; the person might just be shy, or this might be a cultural difference. This is the most commonly frowned-upon handshake as it gives the impression that the person does not want to connect.
- If the person shakes your hand without stopping, place your free hand on top of his hand to indicate that it's time to stop.
- If the person does not extend his hand back after you extend yours to shake, it is OK—you did nothing wrong. You were a business professional,

and the visitor might have something against handshakes.

Always keep your right hand free of folders, bags, glasses, phones, and tissues in order to appear clean and ready to give a good, dry handshake. When you use the restroom, make sure to dry your hands properly, as you never know who you will meet on the way out.

The key idea is to shake neither too softly nor too tightly. You do not want to come across as a pushover nor as aggressive.

INTRODUCING YOURSELF

What do you say to introduce yourself?

It seems so easy to introduce yourself that you seldom think of preparing.

"Good morning, my name is Mark Peters. I am a consultant at Business Etiquette Consultants."

Do you say *Mark* or *Mr. Peters*—or do you just say *good morning*? Do you have to say who you are and what you do?

Depending on the business you are conducting and what you expect to achieve, a proper introduction of your full name and job position will be of good use. Do not be surprised; some people will forget your name the second it comes out of your mouth. It does not matter. You still have to do it right in the first place.

Do not introduce yourself as Mr. or Mrs. Peters, but use your full name, position, and company (if relevant to the person). You need to make eye contact and not have wandering eyes, as this will seem impersonal. Mind your body language and gestures (see chapter 4) so that you appear professional and not too casual.

Your introduction will confirm or build upon the positive impression you made when you first appeared.

INTRODUCING SOMEONE ELSE

Whom do you introduce first?

When you are introducing people, you need to know which one is of the highest importance—for you, which one you want to impress the most. You have then to introduce the person of lesser importance to the one of higher importance.

For example, if you have to introduce two persons of different ranks in the same company, you would say, "Mr. John Peter, (group CEO), let me introduce you to Mr. Marc Philips, head of operations."

On the other hand, if you have to introduce a new client to your CEO, never forget that importance has to be given to your customer: "Mr. Ashimizo, let me introduce you to Mr. John Peter, our CEO."

Do not forget:

- When introducing two persons to each other, ensure that the introduction contains enough relevant information to avoid an uncomfortable silence (company, title, role, etc.). It will help to start the conversation.
- Make sure you get your facts right; do not introduce Mr. Peter as the CFO when he is the CEO.

- Avoid cracking jokes that can embarrass someone during the introduction, as you may lose credibility.
- Once you have conducted the introduction, ensure that you do not become the speaker for both parties. Know when to exit.
- Take time to make a good introduction; do not speak too quickly, but have a good and clear voice.

SPEAKING UP SO YOU CAN BE HEARD

When you greet people and introduce yourself or others, make sure you speak to be heard.

You want your message to be loud and clear. It is very uncomfortable to have to ask someone to repeat himself or herself more than once because he or she speaks softly.

During a seminar we gave, one well-dressed gentleman declared that he does not talk much because he feels that his English is not good. While we conversed, we realized it was not his English but his shyness that was the issue. Not only did he avoid talking to people, but when he did speak, he spoke softly. More than once, he had been asked to repeat himself.

Just tell yourself that if you do not speak up, someone else might get the limelight for saying out loud what you said in a low voice.

Speak up, talk to be heard, talk to be understood. Just as you can practice your handshake, you can practice speaking louder and more clearly.

KISSING AND HUGGING

In a business meeting, never greet a new business partner or a longtime acquaintance with a kiss in front of a crowd. Kisses are reserved for a more social environment.

Kissing and hugging are not common practices in business. However, in a situation where a business associate from another culture approaches you to give a kiss, do not back away. Go with the flow so that you can put your visitor at ease, but do not initiate a kiss. Different cultures, different routines.

In today's business world where women are as active and hardworking as men, we do not usually consider gender in business practices; however, it can be frowned upon to greet a woman with a kiss or hug, depending on the culture.

On the way to the office one morning, a male colleague and I ran into one of our clients. He greeted my colleague with a handshake. I extended my hand, but he ignored it and approached to greet me with a kiss on the cheek. Although I was not at ease with this situation, I had to go along with it, as backing away would have created an awkward situation.

2

Your Look

You spend a few minutes looking at yourself in the mirror daily. However, if you think it through, you'll recognize that other people who you cross in the street or at your workplace become your unreflective mirror. They see you—but without sending your reflection back, very often keeping it to themselves. They see your perfect hairstyle, your flawless makeup, your impeccable hygiene, and your good humor. Nevertheless, it goes without saying that, as human beings, they will also see your negligence.

It is inevitable, upon meeting someone for the first time, that you will make a judgment in the first few seconds. His or her manner of dress, colors of clothing, corpulence, facial expressions, smell, and handshake will determine your opinion—whether you will like or dislike the person. And vice versa, he or she will be judging you too. The eyes have spoken; a silent message has been sent.

Very often, people think that the importance of personal image is a modern concept. In fact, image has always been very important. In 1500 BCE, Egyptians were already taking care of their looks using different clothes, fabrics, jewels, and even wigs.

"It is impossible to wear clothes without transmitting social signals. Every suit, uniform, costume tells a story, often a very subtle one, about the wearer. Even those people who insist that they despise attention to clothing and dress as casually as possible are making quite specific comments on their social roles and their attitude toward the culture in which they live" (Desmond Morris, *Peoplewatching*).

Even if you are wearing a uniform, you cannot escape the importance of projecting a good image. Your uniform will help others identify your role, but the way you wear the uniform will guide others about the type of person you are.

BUSINESS LOOK

You have to be aware of the impact of your look and make sure you use it to your advantage. Your first business card is you; through your look, you tell others who you are.

Posture, attire, gestures, voice, smell, and colors worn will demonstrate your personality more than long speeches.

Be careful not to be a fashion victim, and do not become too addicted to following trends. Before you follow fashion, you have to be sure that the colors, shapes, and styles fit you. You can remain authentic and elegant with simplicity and still be able to respect the business attire of your professional position. Dressing professionally will help give you more credibility, which can positively impact your success, especially when the competitors around you are fierce.

In finding professional attire, it's important for you to find the right balance of what suits you and what feels comfortable.

Some people state that they wear clothes that are too large because they are comfortable. Then again, others wear a size ten when they should be wearing a size twelve. And then you have those who look impeccable in their business suits.

The CEO of a big recruitment firm shared his experience of conducting interviews. He had law graduates coming for interviews, and he was surprised at how many of them were wearing suits that were either too big or too small for them. To him, this came across as unprofessional, as they not only did not look presentable, but they also did not look confident and at ease.

Often, people wear clothes that are too big due to a lack of knowledge and effort to get fit right in the first place.

It is important to consider that your clothes will help give you a confident look.

POINTERS FOR A CONFIDENT LOOK

Cleanliness: From your shoes to your hair, *cleanliness* and *tidiness* are the keywords. Stain is pain: you can wear a nice suit, but if it has a stain, that could ruin the whole look. Be careful with the odors that your clothes absorb: food, cigarettes, sweat, and other smells. If you are one of the lucky ones who can wear your work clothes more than once a week, ensure that you skip a day before repeating. This will give your clothes the chance to ventilate, and it will ensure that you present a different look in between wears.

Sweat: If you feel that you smell of sweat and have a perspiration problem, do not assume that you are the only one who can smell it. A daily shower and a deodorant adapted to your skin type are needed. Finding the right deodorant might take time. Do not hesitate to talk to your pharmacist, as he or she can assist you with finding the right product. Solutions to reduce heavy sweating or strong perspiration odor exist. Having the right product is one step, but washing your clothes after each usage is also very much required.

Cigarette smell: Be careful of the cigarette smell. When you smoke, you have the cigarette smell left on your breath, clothes, hair, and fingers. The more you smoke, the more the cigarette smell remains. This smell can disturb others. If you cannot afford to let go of the cigarettes during your business hours, be strategic with your cigarettes breaks. Go for a smoke when you have enough time to wash your hand and mouth, grab a mint, and freshen your clothes. If you are a smoker, ensure you ventilate your clothes and coats daily. Wash your hair daily, as your hair captures smell. If you are a nonsmoker, avoid standing in front of someone smoking or being in a crowded, enclosed smoking area (for instance, designated smoking areas), as your clothes and hair are also absorbing the cigarette smell.

Other odors: Bad smell is not only linked to perspiration or cigarettes. Watch out for food smells if you do not ventilate your clothes and your living space. If you have animals and you spend a lot of time with them, you will have to wash your clothes and hair more often. If you have a bad smell, people will tend to avoid you. (It will not be your charming personality they are avoiding but your smell.)

Many people love perfume. What you all have to be careful of is wearing too much perfume, which can be distracting for others. If you are not sure if your perfume is too strong, do not hesitate to ask your close acquaintances. Should you be warned about it, go easy on the perfume or change it.

Breath: Brush your teeth more than once a day. Some bad breath may require that you seek professional help. If you think you have bad breath, do something about it (eat a mint, brush your teeth). Do not suppose that others will not smell it; it's possible that they will just be too embarrassed to tell you. If you have bad breath, people will tend to avoid you. (It will not be your charming personality they are avoiding but your breath.)

Tidiness: Your clothes should be neat, with no buttons missing and no threads hanging. When you tuck your shirt in, ensure that it remains tucked in and does not partially stick out—and the same goes for your collar. Ensure you are wearing clothes that are fully ironed. When ironing, watch out for the collar.

Shower: Before you start your day, have a shower. A shower is a must not only for hygiene reasons but also to wake you up and mentally prepare you for the day.

Shoes: Your shoes should be clean and waxed at all time. Shoes are an essential part of your attire; do not neglect them. During our seminars, members of both genders have claimed that they pay attention to the other gender's shoes. It is sometimes normal to leave home with clean shoes and arrive at your destination with dirty or scuffed shoes. Pay attention, and ensure that you clean them on the spot when needed.

Nails: It is important for both genders to have clean and maintained nails. Nails do not necessarily need to be colored to show that they are taken care of. Your nails should be clean and of an even length (as much as possible). Use oil or cream adapted for cuticles to care for dry hands. If you use nail vanish, please ensure that it is refreshed regularly to avoid a neglected and chipped look. Reserve joyous, bright colors (pink, orange, blue, violet, and green) along with nail designs and piercings for holidays or leisure times.

A green or blue nail varnish with a lily painted on it, for example, is not only an uncommon practice in business, but it can also distract the person you are trying to woo and send a childish message.

Avoid biting your nails or the skin around them, as this shows signs of anxiety and stress.

Patrick had just been promoted to a new marketing position. He was now invited to meetings. When he was not talking in the meeting, he was spending his time biting his nails and cuticles. Not only did other participants find that repulsive and disruptive, but they also all realized the intense stress he was under. Less than a year after, Patrick got dismissed, one of the reason being that he couldn't deal with pressure.

Hair: Again, your hair should be clean and tidy. Regular hair washing is needed during the week for both genders. Hair should be cared for before the start of your day and might need a touch-up during the day, depending on the style. If you do not care for your hair properly before the start of your day, you will end up with a neglected look that will ruin your whole professional image. A lot of people notice unkempt hair. Ladies, if you do not want to spend a lot of time with the hairbrush and hair straightener, opt for a bun or ponytail; these give a neater look and often take less time.

Before venturing into hair coloring, please seek professional help to select the right color to your tone as well as ensure even coloring. A poor hair coloring might leave you with very dry hair, which can be difficult to style.

If you are a smoker, washing your hair daily is a must to remove the smoke scent.

Should you be suffering from skin conditions that give you visible dandruff, ensure you refresh yourself continuously by removing the dandruff from your clothes. Gray-colored shirts or suits are better adapted to hiding this condition than darker materials.

Bag/Folder: Your bag or folder should be clean and tidy from the outside. It should not show signs of age and wear. It should be appropriate to the style of clothing you wear. If you are going hiking, having a backpack is totally appropriate. However, if you are in a business suit, a backpack is totally inappropriate, despite its numerous benefits. It is a faux pas and indicates a lack of taste.

Jewelry: Do not wear too much jewelry. Keep it to a minimum. For example, one necklace, a bracelet, or one or two rings (wedding band excluded) are acceptable.

Smile: A smile can make you come across as a sympathetic person. It can turn a tedious situation into one easier to cope with. A genuine smile reaches both your lips and your eyes. A fake smile gives movement to your mouth only; it does not look sincere and can often be detected.

LADIES: BUSINESS LOOK

Your attire says a lot about you. It defines your personality and shows your professionalism. It can also show the respect you have for a person, event, or firm.

It is important to reserve a professional image for your professional environment and a personal image for your private or social environments. Excessively short skirts, low tops, tight clothes, and outfits that reveal your navel—as well as frilly, sexy, or transparent garments—should be reserved for your social or seductive environment.

Your dress or skirt should be neither too long nor too short; it must be adapted to the length of your legs and calves. Choose a suitable length to cover the less-attractive parts of your legs. It is also very important to adapt the length of your skirt to the height of your heels. In the business world, the higher your shoes, the longer the skirt should be, and the shorter the skirt, the smaller the heels should be.

Here are more tips for ladies:

- To look professional, it is imperative to wear a jacket and stockings at all times and in every season, even in summer. Stockings and jackets are now made in thinner versions to adapt to the changes of season.

- If you wear thigh-high stockings, sit down before leaving the house to ensure that the garters do not show when you sit down or cross your legs. Ensure the stockings stay up well and are not losing elasticity. Ladies, always have a second pair of stocking in your bag. You never know when your stockings might break, and there is nothing worse than a torn stocking. Leave the net stockings for private or social moments.
- Bear in mind that stockings do not necessarily hide unshaven legs.
- Ensure that no lingerie or labels are visible when you are sitting down or standing up in your business environment.
- Always match the colors in your attire; do not exceed three colors at the same time. The more discreet you are with your suit, the better it will be for your authority and credibility. You should also consider adding colorful accessories (such as a scarf, a pin, and necklace). Be aware that in different parts of the world, such as Asia, different colors have different meanings (e.g., wearing a red suit is for good luck).
- The right touch of makeup always has a positive impact. It gives you a healthier look. Your day makeup should be discreet and not too flashy. Colorful eye shadows are reserved for evenings. Wearing blush without foundation is incomplete; wearing

mascara without foundation is incomplete; wearing foundation without a gloss or lipstick is incomplete. If you do not know how to apply your day makeup, there are doubtlessly many services available nearby to guide you.

- A proper day makeup should look natural. It should even out your skin tone but not change it. Be careful not to leave any makeup traces on your clothes.

My husband and I were invited to an event where we were introduced to another female guest. She was wearing a white top with a high collar. She had chosen a foundation color darker than her skin, so she had put on the foundation down to her neckline. Unfortunately, during the event, the makeup had smudged onto her white collar. It was not a nice scene, especially since she was not aware of it.

- Watch out for lipstick traces on your teeth.

Elegance is achieved by paying attention to the little, minor details.

GENTLEMEN: BUSINESS LOOK

It is a true statement that women have more choices of clothes than men. It is still surprising to see the common faux pas that men commit with business attire. A suit without its matching shoes, socks, belt, and accessories can ruin the whole image.

During our seminars, we have raised the question of whether men's shoes are important in completing business attire. Most participants reported putting great importance on gentlemen's shoes, especially ladies. Dirty or old shoes send a bad image and do not make a good impression. However, nice, clean shoes send a positive image. A man wearing matching shoes, socks, and belt is considered rare and impressive.

Your formal business attire is made of three different pieces: your suit, your shirt, and your tie. If you wish to wear stripes or other patterns, ensure that only one of these three pieces bears the patterns. It is advisable that the two other pieces are of solid colors, as wearing multiple patterns can be visually distracting.

Other advice for gentlemen:

- Long socks are important to avoid showing your skin when crossing your legs.

- Choose your socks with care. Be careful that they are not losing their color or elasticity. Your socks, shoes, and belt should be of the same color. Those who risk playing with colors should have the posture and confidence that go with that choice.
- It is a total fashion faux pas to wear short sleeves with a tie. Lighter-fabric shirts with long sleeves can be found and worn during warmer temperatures.
- To know if your sleeves are of the right length, be aware that they should extend approximately one to two centimeters beyond the jacket sleeves and be visible.
- Traditional shirts are made to be worn with a tie. If you are dressed in a business-casual outfit and the tie is not mandatory, a high-collar shirt is preferable. If you wear a T-shirt under your shirt, ensure that it is not visible.
- Your keys, phone, wallet, pack of cigarettes, and the rest are to be banned from your pockets. Not only do they not flatter your silhouette, but these bulky items will enlarge and deform your pockets, and with time, the keys might put holes in your pockets. Carry what you need in your hand and leave the rest in your bag or in the office.
- A backpack is useful, as it is easier to carry and to transport documents in than a briefcase; however, it is not suitable when you are wearing business

attire. Complete your business image with a proper business bag, a slim bag, or a shoulder bag.

- Companies' dress codes often request that males wear minimum jewelry. Limit your jewelry to the traditional pieces: tie accent, watch, cuff links, wedding band, and signet ring. If you want to wear your favorite chain, ensure that it is hidden under your shirt and not resting over your tie. In many strict business environments where a suit is requested, piercings are not acceptable and do not send a good message. Remember, if you need to earn people's trust, piercings or visible tattoos can ruin your hard work and credibility.

- If you wear cuff links, remember to keep them simple. You will unlikely get it wrong with simplicity, but you might get it wrong with extravagance.

- To know the right length to tie your tie, note that the widest part (the tip), should hang roughly at the edge of your belt or the waistband of your trousers. Should your tie fall above your belt or far below your waistband, you did it wrong. Avoid flashy or illustrated ties in a serious business environment.

- Depending on your company's policy, facial hair may or may not be authorized. Very often, this policy is based on what kind of image the company wants to project. In the hospitality industry, facial hair is often not permitted—for hygiene purposes but also to give an impression of meticulous care and respect for the customers. It is becoming trendier to have a three-day well-maintained beard. If your company allows facial hair, for the customer's sake but more importantly your own, ensure that you have a nice consistent growth, as this will give a cleaner and tidier effect. The opposite option leaves holes and a messy look and puts focus on the fact that you do not have a full growth.

BUSINESS COLORS

Choose the color of your business attire with care. Take into consideration the type of message you want to send.

Dark colors (black, navy, or charcoal gray, with or without stripes) are commonly used because they send out a more serious message and demonstrate more authority. Everyone can wear dark colors and look good in them. Another advantage of dark colors is that they can be worn in every occasion.

Lighter colors send a friendlier and warmer message. These groups of colors do not necessarily suit every skin tone or hair type. Compared to darker colors, lighter ones cannot be worn in every occasion.

Nevertheless, do not be too dark in your attire; use your shirt or accessories to boost the whole outfit. Be careful not to mix more than three colors at the same time, and avoid matching colors that are too similar, unless you have the confidence required to do so.

3

Impressions

> *Elegance is not about being noticed, it is about being remembered.*
>
> — GIORGIO ARMANI

During business interactions, it is crucial to make a good impression straightaway. Although we are all told to never judge a book by its cover, this is exactly what humans do unconsciously. It is a survival mechanism that influences your opinions and the ways you interact with others.

Your nonverbal communication will heavily impact your **first impression.** As stated by the psychologist Michael Argyle, "the non-verbal communication is twelve times more powerful than the verbal, in other words you see more than you hear." Therefore, know whom you are going to meet and what kind of environment you are going to be meeting in. Making a good impression is not only important when you think you are being watched but under all circumstances. This is because:

- You never know who is watching you.
- You never know who you are dealing with.
- You never know who can make a difference in your life.
- You never know who you might meet.

I remember working at a company where I had to carry out internal recruitment among students. I had to select fifteen candidates from a pool of sixty. As I was new to the company, the students did not know who I was. Through my observations, I realized that some of these candidates totally disregarded me when I passed them in the corridor. There were no greetings, no consideration for me. What was interesting to observe was the change in attitude after the interview to a more considerate and polite manner.

In order to make a good first impression, it is imperative to know where you are going, who you are meeting, and what the aim of this encounter is. A good first impression requires that you pay attention to your personal presentation, adapted to the occasion and the environment.

You need to work on having a confident posture without seeming arrogant or too relaxed.

Your facial expression needs to be adapted to the situation.

Very often, a lot of emphasis is put on those first few seconds you have to make a good first impression and on how you do not have a second chance. Does that mean that, once the first good impression is made, you can rest and take it easy?

MAINTAINING THE FIRST IMPRESSION

Once you have worked to make that good first impression, it is very important to maintain it during your later interactions. Adopt the right manners and use good etiquette tools.

During your encounters, do not become too familiar nor too comfortable because the pressure has been released. Always be on your guard and stay respectful and professional. Show interest, be a good listener, and know what you are talking about.

While maintaining a good impression, get people to see more positive sides of you. Throughout this book, you will find useful information in all chapters that will help you achieve this.

LAST IMPRESSION

Your last impression is as important as your first. When it is time to exit, make sure to do it in a graceful and polite way. Do not put great effort into making and maintaining a good impression, only to ruin it when leaving. Say *good-bye* and show your appreciation for the encounter, regardless of the outcome of your meeting.

Your last impression can make up for your prior imperfections.

LASTING IMPRESSIONS

What others remember of you after you leave is your lasting impression. At this phase, you do not have much control over what they think of you; however, you can push them in the right direction by writing them a thank-you note. You want people to remember you for the right reasons. Working on your impressions will help to get you there.

Just because the outcome of your encounter did not meet your expectations, this does not mean that you were not noticed. What is important is to leave a good impression of yourself in general.

A good image can never replace a professional qualification, but it can help you to reach your goals.

During a meeting or conversation, your partner retains

7 percent of your words **(VERBAL)**
38 percent of your voice **(VOCAL)**
55 percent of your image **(VISUAL)**, including clothes, posture, gestures, facial expressions
(Albert Mehrabian, *Silent Messages*, Wadsworth Publishing: Belmont, California).

4

Nonverbal Communication

BODY LANGUAGE

What is your body saying that your voice is not?

Body language, also known as *kinesics*, is a very useful tool in communication, a powerful concept that more and more successful people are putting into practice. It is considered to be a significant part of modern communication, and it plays an important role in relationships.

When intentions, thoughts, or feelings are expressed through physical behaviors, this is considered nonverbal communication. During verbal communication, a lot of talking and listening are involved, whereas in nonverbal communication it is important to pay attention to posture, gestures, eye movements, the use of space (proxemics), and touch. Throughout this chapter you will receive a few tips regarding nonverbal communication.

Watch out for the way you walk, stand, shake hands, make eye contact, smile, move your hands, make micro-movements, cross your legs, and leave space between you and your guest.

Your body language can show confidence, friend-liness, or honesty. It can also show shyness, stress, or foibles. Through your body language, you send out mes-sages about your personality. Are you a warm and wel-coming or a strict and distant person?

Your body language will reveal your true emotions to others, and other people's body language will reveal their feelings to you.

Sending and receiving body-language signals hap-pens on a conscious or unconscious basis, even if you try hard to dissimulate your real feelings.

When the nonverbal contradicts the verbal, only then will a person's nonverbal radar become more active. When the nonverbal becomes negative or closed, it is important to know how to redirect the situation to your advantage.

Watch out for clichéd or false interpretations of body language, as these can cause you to jump too fast to a conclusion. You do not want to create misunderstandings and miss out on opportunities.

The beauty of mastering body language, at least minimally, is that it will help you understand the dissimilarities between verbal and nonverbal communication. It will be easier for you to comprehend your customers and colleagues. It will be a useful tool to know when you have won, lost, impressed, or offended other people.

Remember, knowledge of body language is not only useful to read other people but also to know yourself better. Give yourself credibility by improving your weaknesses and sending a positive image of yourself.

POSTURE

You smile, you are nice, but no one talks to you. You do not understand why. What does your posture say about you? Why does your colleague or friend have more success with strangers than you? If you have asked yourself these questions in your private or professional life, you should observe the colleague or friend in question.

How does he or she stand? How do you stand? What do you do with your hands? What does he or she do with his or her hands? These are the things you can observe that can help you understand your colleague's success before even analyzing his or her verbal conversation.

Your posture should project confidence. To achieve that, you should have a straight, unhunched posture with your head up but with no arrogance. A good guide to a straight posture is to use the old-fashioned technique of walking with a book balanced on your head.

A hunched posture shows a lack of confidence or a closed personality.

SITTING

Your use of space on a chair, the direction you turn, and the amount of time you move forward or backward while seated will give people an indication of your interest in what they are saying. Likewise, paying attention to other people's posture will help you notice if you have caught or lost their attention.

For example, while you speak, if the listener leans toward you, there might be a chance that you have caught his attention. You therefore want to develop the subject of the conversation further to heighten your advantage. If, on the other hand, the person leans back on his chair, there is a chance that the subject is not to his liking; hence, if you want to win him back, you might want to change the subject.

Depending on what you want to achieve during your conversation, these two simple chair positions might give you an indication of when you have impacted someone negatively or positively.

If your listener keep leaning into his chair, his body pulled away from you, and if he is fidgeting, you will want to take a break by offering him something to drink or by asking questions that will encourage him to talk. Observing his facial expression will give you good indication of his level of interest as well.

The direction that the person crosses his legs can also be a good indicator of his state of mind. Which way is he crossing his legs? If his knees are pointing toward you, there is a good chance that he is comfortable and at ease. The opposite does not mean that he is uncomfortable, but it might mean that you have to work a bit harder to gain his trust.

If someone is sitting at the edge of the chair, this is not a positive sign; it shows that he is ready to leave the conversation. Your challenge will be to make this person feel comfortable enough to remain in the conversation before jumping to the core of the subject.

HANDS ARE TALKING

It is very easy to resort to clichés when observing and analyzing hands. Often during interviews, human-resources departments tend to put too much focus on candidates' hands only. We all remember that, in the story of Bill Clinton and Monica Lewinsky, when he denied the affair on national television, Bill Clinton touched his nose. Since that episode, you have heard and will continue to hear that when you touch your nose, it means you are not telling the truth.

What you did not realize was that, when Bill Clinton touched his nose, the professionals were observing more than just his hands and his nose. They took into consideration his hunched posture, his lack of eye contact during certain sentences, his head position, his twitch, the anger shown on his mouth on certain words, and whether he touched his nose with his left or right hand.

Another cliché that a lot of us know about is arm folding. This action does not necessarily mean you are a closed or an unfriendly person, nor that you are necessarily freezing. In order to determine one's state of mind during this action, take into consideration which way the arms are folded. Is the right or left arm on top? Is the palm open or closed in a tight fist? Are the hands well hidden under the armpits? Or is there nothing unusual at this moment with this action?

While observing someone's hands, consider the environment the person is in, what is being said, and other nonverbal gestures before jumping to a conclusion.

Your hands talk a lot. To give a positive and confident image of yourself, avoid the following:

- Putting both hands in your pockets when talking
- Wiping your hands together nonstop
- Pointing your finger toward someone when talking
- Fidgeting with items (pen, hair, glass, napkin)
- Touching your face too frequently
- Scratching your head or other body parts
- Playing with your nails
- Putting your hands behind you
- Keeping your hands in fists
- Tapping your fingers while talking
- Blowing your nose with your right hand (the right hand is reserved for shaking hands; hence, it has to remain clean.)

FEET ARE TALKING

Compared to hands, feet are less complicated. Closed legs and open legs differentiate between a more giving person and a more taking person.

To give a positive, confident image of yourself, avoid the following:

- Crossing your legs when standing
- Putting one foot on top of the other foot when talking
- Taking too much space by spreading legs too far apart
- Leaning your foot on a nearby wall
- Tapping your legs when talking
- Showing the soles of your shoes when crossing your legs

Ladies, for more elegance, keep your legs close together.

Gentlemen, do not take too much space when seated.

GESTURES

Some gestures are easy to comprehend no matter the age or the continent; thus, they can facilitate communication. When you wave your hand to say *hello* or *good-bye* to someone, this message is universal.

Some gestures are easy to identify without being a body language expert; however, some can be more technical, though they remain universal.

Some gestures are done automatically to emphasize a phrase or a feeling. Others contradict speech, betraying contained emotions.

To give a positive, confident image of yourself, avoid the following:

- Touching your nose, eyes, or forehead frequently
- Playing with your hair
- Fidgeting too much with items
- Moving and changing positions on your chair too often
- Biting your nails
- Crossing and uncrossing your arm and legs
- Straightening your clothes frequently
- Straightening your tie during the conversation
- Wiping imaginary dust off the table or your clothes
- Biting your pen, glasses, or other items

- Biting your lips
- Compressing your lips
- Being too illustrative when you are describing something

Research to improve the understanding of nonverbal communication is ongoing. Some gestures have different meanings depending on the culture. For example, the meaning of a vertical head shake differs from China to Greece, from Greece to India, and from India to the rest of Europe.

Therefore, a little advice: the fewer gestures you make, the more impact your verbal communication will have, as there will be nothing else to read.

MICROEXPRESSIONS

Each emotion triggers a unique series of signals that affect body language, voice, speech, and expressions.

If you have ever watched the series *Lie to Me*, inspired by Paul Ekman's work, you have a global idea of microexpressions. It is said that microexpressions are quick and intense facial expressions that reveal your real emotions. Very often, microexpressions can go by unnoticed, thus the difficulty of really seeing someone's genuine feelings. You can play with your words and gestures, but your microexpressions can betray you, as they are movements that you cannot control.

Microexpressions have been grouped into seven universal emotions:

Happiness is seen when the person has a genuine smile, giving wrinkles around the eyes. The cheeks are lifted, and the corners of the lips are turned upward.

Sadness is observed when the upper eyelids are dropped. The corners of the lips are turned downward, and the eyes have no focus.

Contempt is seen when a person is concealing self-satisfaction or exhibiting superiority. The lips tighten, and only one side of the lips is lifted.

Disgust is observed when the upper lip is raised, sometimes displaying the teeth. The nose is wrinkled.

Surprise is seen when the eyes are wide open, causing the eyelids and eyebrows to be lifted. The mouth is dropped open for a few seconds.

Fear is observed when the eyebrows and upper eyelids are pulled up, causing wrinkles on the forehead. Tension is seen on the lower eyelids, and the lips are stretched.

Anger is seen when the person has tightened lips. The nostrils flare, and the eyebrows are pulled down toward the nose. The eyes are in a constant or persistent stare.

Learn the meanings of your own expressions; you will, in turn, begin to recognize those of others'.

THE SMILE

Smiling is a learned phenomenon that people pick up long before they are able to express themselves with verbal or sign language. Smiling influences other people's attitudes and reactions toward you.

Your smile will help determine if you will be considered a friendly and warm person or the contrary. Your smile will alert others if you are nervous or at ease. Your smile will also define your approachability. As little and unimportant as the smile may seem to be, it is an action with great impact. A smile always lights up a face.

Smiles are classified into two categories:

A genuine smile involves the whole face, more than just the mouth, and many facial muscles are in action. The muscles tightening around the eyes are the most visible. This action around the eyes is extremely difficult to fake and is the main signal that will help you identify someone's genuine smile.

A camera smile involves smiling only with the mouth. It is a polite smile that a person feels is needed to get him or her by. It is often seen when people are posing for a picture, greeting someone, or trying to make a sale. Very often, a camera smile can be recognized by others. Thus, using a camera smile, you will often not achieve your goal.

How many times have you entered a service area and been greeted by a smiling salesperson, only to realize that the smile disappears once the person turns away from you?

A genuine smile lasts longer on your face, as there are more muscles involved compared to a camera smile. A genuine smile can easily lead to laughter.

To project a genuine smile when you do not feel like it, think of a pleasant memory that always brings a smile to your face.

EYE CONTACT

In certain parts of the world, not establishing eye contact can be seen as an offense; however, in other parts, looking someone in the eyes, especially someone of a superior rank, can be seen as disrespectful and offensive. How do you manage to make the right choice in a globalized, fast-paced world?

When we have asked people, *How do you feel when someone addresses you without eye contact?* a lot of people have stated that it seems impersonal, but others reported that they are not bothered by it, as they are uncomfortable looking people straight in the eyes.

When establishing eye contact, do not stare fiercely, as this can be unsettling. A tip is to look at the person in the middle of his forehead. It does not give the impression that you are staring into the person's eyes, nor does it directly indicate that you are not making eye contact. If someone is not giving you eye contact, take into consideration his or her cultural background before jumping to a conclusion, as this person might be making false conclusions about you for looking at him or her in the eyes.

Looking at someone's left eye with your left eye is a way to establish conversation in a soft, friendly manner. You want to meet his or her eye with your right eye when giving orders. This observation can be made of a mother with her child; she will tend to use her left eye when looking at her child. Conversely, a boss who is unhappy with you and who is expecting results will tend to look at your right eye with his. Looking at one eye or the other is an action that is carried out automatically, depending on the situation you are faced with. It is not easy to control. Through practice and observation, you will become more aware of it and can then use it wisely.

To conclude this chapter, under no circumstances is it acceptable to conduct business while wearing your sunglasses. Remember to remove it from resting on your head as well.

PROXEMICS

Edward T. Hall defined *proxemics* as the way people use physical space in interpersonal interaction.

He described the most important aspect of proxemics as the use of personal territory. The four areas of personal territory are public, social, personal, and intimate.

Public space is considered to be the distance maintained between the audience and a speaker such as the President.

Social space is considered to be the distance used for communication among business associates, as well as to separate strangers using public areas. Think of it as an arm length.

Personal space ranges is the distance used among friends and family members, and to separate people queueing. Think of this distance as not really have to stretch your arm to touch someone.

Intimate space is normally involves a high probability of touching. It is reserve for whispering and embracing.

Personal territories, however, can vary both culturally and ethnically. Take Saudi Arabia for example, you might find yourself almost nose to nose with a business associate because their social space equates to our intimate space. You would probably find yourself backing away trying to regain your social space while your associate pursues you across the floor trying to maintain his. Finally, you would come away from the encounter thinking he was pushy, and he would come away thinking you were standoffish.

If, on the other hand, you were visiting a friend in the Netherlands, you would find the roles reversed, you would be doing the chasing because their personal space equates to our social space.

Major aspects that can affect our interactions with others are cultural differences, use of color in our physical environment, eye-contact, facial expression, smells, body warmth, gender, number of people involved, subject matter, and goals of the communication, for which you will continuously and automatically adjust the use of space. (Edward T. Hall. *The Hidden Dimension.*)

Often in our seminars, it is brought to our attention that the issue in regards to proxemics is the invasion of personal territories during a conversation or networking opportunity. A piece of advice, when you feel that you cannot

stand the closeness of someone, performing large gestures with your hands while talking will make the person
automatically move backward.

5

Customer Service

IS IT ENOUGH TO HAVE TECHNICAL SKILLS?

In today's business world, conducting business with excellence is a daily challenge. Customers' demands and competitors' continuous growth require that all companies possess more than just the technical skills.

Companies must be more customer-service oriented to achieve their goals and enjoy long-term success. Delivering quality customer service is as important as providing the best products and know-how. Each customer who uses your business as a service provider deserves your best service to ensure loyalty. This is one of the keys to creating the repeated-customer effect.

Properly established customer service will increase your return on investment, cut your costs, give your company credibility, and heighten your positive image, as well as give you an advantage over your competitors.

Satisfied and happy customers bring you free advantageous publicity by giving others recommendations. Unsatisfied customers can negatively impact your business, tarnishing your reputation and affecting your company's growth in the long term.

How do you create happy customers and influence them to remain loyal?

KEEP AND CHASE YOUR CUSTOMER

My hairdresser had to choose which supplier she preferred between two. She realized that the first supplier only contacted her when he needed money and that he was not always on time. The second supplier would contact her often to check if she was satisfied with the order, not to mention that they were always prompt when delivering. Which company do you think she chose to work with?

When people walk into your business, they want to try your product. Your service has to be impeccable, as you want customers to come again along with their friends and family—and the friends and family of their friends and family.

If at first they do not purchase your service, you still have to leave them with the impression that you are the best, so they will come back.

WOW: BEYOND EXPECTATION

I was late with my Christmas gift shopping, as usual. I called this store to find out if they had a specific item I wanted for my husband. Over the phone, the salesgirl was absolutely empathetic. An hour later, I was at the store. As promised, the salesgirl had kept my item. With absolute kindness, she took care of my demand, acknowledged the presence of my sons, and ensured that I had all the necessary information for the good usage of the item. Once my purchase was done, she even offered to keep my shopping bag, so I could be more comfortable while I tended to the rest of my errands.

Days, weeks, months later, this store still sends us handwritten invitations to their events as well as updates on their new products.

I left the shop with a big smile and a feeling of amazement, not only because I got what I came in for but because the service was beyond my expectations. This was the place I would go the next time I wanted to buy a similar item. This experience I have shared and will share with people around me who are looking for this kind of product or an idea for a gift.

To give service beyond expectations, you have to anticipate your customers' demands. Make the difference with little things and attention with a positive attitude.

CAN I CHOOSE MY CUSTOMER?

We are a couple of handbag fanatics. On one of our business trip, we decided to stop at a handbag store. For one reason or another, the saleslady decided we were not worth paying attention to and ignored us. We decided to observe if, with time, she was going to change and give us a little bit of attention. To our surprise, she stood there with a very severe attitude and did not budge. We ended up apologizing to her for having walked into her shop, and we conducted our business somewhere else.

A client who does not purchase today might purchase tomorrow. The kind of scenario that happened in the legendary film *Pretty Woman* should be ancient history. In the movie, Julia Roberts's character received appalling service because she did not have the profile of the store's regular customers. Thus, she became the customer of the competitor.

Unfortunately this scenario does still happen today. Customers need consideration the minute they walk in or call. Do your best to be better than your competitors.

Very often, we do not get to choose our customers—they choose us. If you are among the lucky ones who can afford to be picky with your customers, do it with tact and diplomacy, as the wheel turns. You might not need those customers today, but they might have an impact on your business tomorrow with their recommendations to the people they know.

What have been your good and bad experiences with customer service?

6

Networking

Often, management teams across different compa-nies share the same concerns when it comes to net-working. Their staffs tend not to use networking events organized by the companies for their intended purpose. Staff members have a habit of sticking together or always talking to the same people throughout the evening. They tend to consider such events as just more gatherings that keep them from getting home. Instead of taking care of the customers at the event, they use the event to speak to, eat with, and drink with colleagues.

In general, networking can seem complex for these reasons:

- You are not at ease talking to people you do not know.
- You don't know how to begin a conversation.

- You don't how to deal with a very quiet and shy person.
- You are unfamiliar with the topics being discussed.
- You fear rejection.
- You fear disturbing people.
- You are uninterested.
- You feel tired after a day of work.
- You are unable to extricate yourself from an actual conversation.

A networking event needs preparation, both mental and physical. Consider these points if you are planning to attend a networking event:

- What is the event theme?
- What are you going to wear?
- At what time is the event starting?
- What is your objective?
- When should you get there?
- Who will be there?
- Whom do you want to meet?
- Where is the event taking place?
- Where will you be parking?
- How many prospects do you want to talk to?
- How many current clients do you want to talk to?
- How acquainted are you with the location?
- What are your role and importance during the event?

A lack of good preparation will hinder your success and your comfort during the event. The reasons you are not at ease with networking will be the same reasons the people you're there to meet are dreading networking.

Conversing with strangers with ease requires practice. Only by making it a habit will you find it easier and become a savvy networker. Being more active in events organized in your area will help you put your networking skills into practice.

A simple school reunion, for example, will help you to talk to other people without too much at stake, apart from gaining more experience and information. Involving yourself in different associations is another networking opportunity.

Simple and accessible occasions to network occur during your daily activities. As soon as you get out of your home, on your way to work or to the store, you run into people you are either acquainted with or not; they can help you polish your networking skills. A long speech is not necessary; simple greetings and small talk will be good starts to building this habit.

It will happen that a conversation does not turn out as you wish despite your efforts. It is absolutely normal that some people are less talkative for different reasons. Let alone, these people might just not want to converse with you. You are not obliged to appreciate the company of everyone, and not everyone is obliged to converse with you just because you have decided to strike up a conversation. Be smart enough to know when to give up. Another individual might be happy to be in the presence of your company.

Do not underestimate the power of networking and the impact someone can have on your life, even those you think are not worth talking to. You might miss opportunities if you keep to yourself—or gain a lot if you put yourself out there positively.

GETTING INTO A GROUP

Involving yourself in an existing conversation inside a group of people is not as easy as it seems. If you initiate eye contact, someone might physically adjust the group to get you in—but then again, maybe not. So what do you do when you are not invited? Do you just barge in?

Mike, a very talkative colleague, feels he has no problems networking as he is at ease meeting and talking to new people. However, when he enters a group, he has a habit of arriving loudly. Not only does Mike not wait to be invited, but he also comes in and starts his conversation to the detriment of the ongoing one.

If you are trying to join a group but feel that the group is busy conversing and that no one is acknowledging your nearby presence, there is a big chance that, at this precise moment, your presence is not welcome. Do not take it personally; it might be that the conversers are talking about something that they do not want to share. Do not insist—you might be accepted in the group at a later stage.

When you enter a group where people are engaged in a conversation, a smile and a small greeting will do. No need to add to the conversation straightaway. Learn to listen.

BUSINESS CARDS

Your business card is a readable description of what you do. People will use it to gain an insight into your professional capacities. Its purpose is to serve as a marketing tool, a way of attracting customers with the hope that they will connect with you.

An effective business card needs to be straight to the point, attractive, and professional looking.

In today's globalized tech world, you must have a website and an e-mail address on your business card. Your website is where all your detailed information will be. Your business card will be the trigger that will raise people's curiosity to visit your website.

Your card should be of good quality and taste in order to be memorable, especially when you are a small company. You want to stand out from the rest. The quality of your card will reflect the image and type of company you are running or representing.

Your business card must be up to date; you do not want to be saying, "Here is my business card, but I am sorry—let me write my correct phone number, as this one is not working anymore. And this is my e-mail address, since I changed." This does not set a good professional image of yourself.

If your business cards are not properly stored, they will get an untidy look, becoming folded and dirty. The best solution will be to store them in a business-card holder made for this purpose. Your cards should be easily accessible, not requiring you to empty your bag in front of potential customers or associates.

If you receive a business card from someone else, have courtesy and do not just put in your pocket. Your business card holder or wallet can be a good place for it. A business card is someone's investment, both in time and money, so do not accept it as you would a receipt from your grocery store. When you receive a business card from someone else, take time to read it in front of the person. It can be an opening line to a great conversation or relationship.

SMALL TALK AND BIG SUCCESS

Small talk might seem insignificant, yet its effect can be big. Professional and personal relationships have been established through small talk. When you develop a habit of doing small talk, it becomes natural.

To involve yourself in small talk, establish eye contact. Eye contact will be the start of your conversation. A friendly and approachable attitude is also needed to put both you and the other person at ease.

How do you start a conversation? Do you introduce yourself, or do you talk about the weather? What do you say about yourself when you do your introduction? Do you say enough? Are you speaking too much? Are you being heard and understood? Make sure to keep the conversation light; it has to be an exchange of words rather than a monologue.

Just because you are a big fan of football, that does not mean your guest is too. Be careful to find out if this topic is of interest to your companion before launching yourself into the discussion. If the person is not really responsive about the subject you have started, do not go deeper.

Here are a few tips to get small talk started:

- Avoid interrupting and finishing someone's sentence.
- Avoid gossiping.
- Avoid criticizing.
- Avoid giving your opinion straightaway; get the other person's opinion first.
- Do not fidget with your phone, hair, or clothes when talking.
- Occasionally nod, smile, or say, "I see," or "Really?" to ensure the person feels listened to.
- Rephrase sentences if needed to show you are listening or interested. Rephrasing will also give you and the other person time to breathe and continue.
- Be positive, be respectful, and be smart
- Be a great listener.
- Give compliments (but not overly personal ones, especially to the opposite gender).
- Ask questions.
- Give your full attention.
- Do not make too many jokes (you might not have the same sense of humor).
- Exit with grace by thanking the person and saying *good-bye*.

Do not do small talk only when you are expecting something in return. Doing it every day will give you continuous practice. Your consideration might well be appreciated by others.

> *Christophe, an acquaintance I meet twice or thrice a year, impresses me all the time. He is the kind of person who talks but especially listens with his ears and his heart. Christophe asks the right questions and gets me to talk. Petty things, such as my daily activities, my work, seem of interest to him. Before I know it, I have opened up to him and am involved in a deep conversation. Not only is he good with his choice of words, but his body language sends out a message of sympathy.*

MEETING NEW PEOPLE

How important are your opening lines?

Your opening line will determine the continuation of your encounter. You want to make sure that your opening line does not become your closing line.

Everyone is so busy that it is almost hard to squeeze a conversation in. Make the most of it when you have the opportunity to converse with someone.

If your opening line is a joke that is not considered funny by others in a conversing group, you stand a risk that they will walk away.

OPEN-ENDED AND CLOSED-ENDED QUESTIONS

Asking questions is a way to gather information but also to show an interest in another person. It is important to note that there are two types of questions: closed ended and open ended.

Open-ended questions will create a better connection, as they show care, compassion, and consideration for the person's answer. With an open-ended question, the person has to elaborate on his answer; thus, a conversation can be engaged. Using open-ended questions with introverted people will help and encourage them to open up. Do not ask questions that are too personal, as this can be offensive.

Consider these examples of open-ended questions:

- What did you think of the conference?
- How did you learn about the show?
- Where will the next workshop take place?

If your open-ended questions give you one-word answers, rephrasing what has been said will give you time to ask another question.

Closed-ended questions are easier to ask but evoke less of a response. You will receive a *yes* or a *no* and less elaboration, unless you are faced with a big talker. If you have asked a closed-ended question, follow up with an open-ended one. Use closed-ended questions when you want to get a direct answer.

Take these examples of closed-ended questions:

- Did you like the show?
- Are you working for this company?
- Would you like some red wine?

ENDING A CONVERSATION

As much as you would like to stay and keep the conversation going, you sometimes have to end the chat for various reasons. Your other commitments or your lack of interest will be factors that will influence the length of your conversation.

How do you get out of a conversation without offending anyone and while still retaining a lasting positive impression?

In the event that there are other acquaintances around during a one-on-one conversation, eye contact can bring another person to your duo. You can then exit after you have introduced the newcomer, and the possibility of a conversation between the two of them has been established.

If you are in a group, your exit will be easier, as most of the time the conversation can continue without you, and the other people will not be left alone.

Knowledge of body language will help you notice is a conversation partner wants to leave.

If none of the above seem to be helping, consider these other exit strategies:

- "It's been nice talking to you. Please excuse me. I have to meet someone."
- "Excuse me for a minute. I will be back."
- "I am going to get some food or drinks. I will be back."
- "Excuse me, I have to make an important phone call. It has been nice talking to you."
- "I did not see time flying. I have to leave, but it was great talking to you."
- "I have to leave. Can we meet again to continue this talk?"

When you are leaving, wrap up the conversation; don't just leave abruptly. A smile and expression of your gratitude for the time spent is a graceful way of exiting.

TOPICS

How is your wife doing?

Unless you are very close to a person and well aware of his or her life happenings, avoid being too familiar straightaway when trying to engage in a conversation.

In order to establish a new business, Lea had to call an old business relation she hadn't talked to in years. When she called, before talking about business straightaway, she engaged in small talk.

The first question she asked was, "How is your wife?" Unfortunately for her, she didn't know that her business relation was in the middle of a complicated divorce.

The relation saw in Lea a shoulder to cry on. The conversation regarding the divorce and the wife lasted an hour. Lea was therefore unable to talk about business during that phone call.

The second time she called, she felt obliged to ask how he was doing, and again the conversation turned into a private one, as it seemed the relation had found in Lea a good listener.

Asking about family seems harmless but can be hurtful if the family is going through some unfortunate situation.

Not only might the person close up, but you might find yourself in an awkward situation.

When you involve yourself in a topic, know what you are talking about. Know your subject. You do not want to talk about the game if you know nothing about football.

Professional networkers have for habit of taking mental or written notes of the conversations they have as a way of giving importance to the people they want to flatter the next time they speak. For example, they could later ask, "So how was your son's match last month?"

Stay broad in choosing topics:

- Weather: "It has been snowing a lot here—how is it on your side?"
- Sports: "What did you think of the game last night?"
- Reality: "I have to start my Christmas shopping—where are you with yours?"
- Events: "Which concerts are you going to attend at the jazz festival?"

Giving your opinion to someone without knowing his first might prevent a conversation from starting. If the person's opinion differs strongly from yours, he might not tell you but silently disagree with you, thus create a blockage to pursuing the conversation further.

If you are really interested in engaging in a conversation with the person, find out what his opinion is. If it differs from yours and you still want to pursue the conversation, be delicate and change the topic to ease the tension.

Often people conduct business over the phone or e-mail, without knowing the person on the other side. When the occasion presents itself to finally meet your business associate face to face, be careful of what you say, as what seems obvious to you might end up putting you in an awkward situation.

Thomas was finally going to meet his elderly clients who was investing in his company. Over the phone his clients often talked about his daughter and her artwork. When his clients arrived in the company of a young lady, Thomas greeted him and added, ' I finally meet your daughter'. Unfortunately for Thomas, it was not his daughter but his new wife.

Avoid such controversial topics as these:

- Sexually oriented conversation
- Religion and events linked to it
- Money and salary
- Expensive leisure
- Politics
- Illness
- A subject you haven't mastered

Over a dinner we were invited to, while we were being asked about Seychelles, someone around the table made an unfortunate joke about how long the Seychelles islands were going to stay above water. Not only did I think his joke was sad and inconsiderate, but I also considered this person to be lacking in intelligence. I did not end up engaging him in serious conversation during the evening.

WHAT DO YOU DO AFTER?

Often people believe that networking ends when you bid farewell to the person or leave the location. The reason you exchange contacts during networking is to have a possibility to stay in touch later.

If you have exchanged business cards with someone, a nice gesture is to send an e-mail or to call the person to thank him for his presence. This will make you come across as thoughtful, kind, and professional. It makes you stand out from the rest. You never know what might come out of it.

To be a person of your word, you have to commit to anything you offered or proposed during the chat. If you gave your word to call or e-mail someone after your encounter, you have to respect it and take action accordingly.

During our workshops, we are often questioned about how long to wait before sending the e-mail or making the call. We recommend that you wait one or two days after the event. After a networking session, people might be busy tending to what they have promised to do, as well as to their daily, routine communications that form part of their jobs. Your e-mail arriving straight after your event might get little attention or become forgotten due to a lack of time. Be careful not to be too pushy or too demanding in your request.

A word of advice if you are expecting a return or an action in response to your communication from a new contact: Friday might not be the best day to send your e-mail.

However, if during your encounter you set a day or time to follow up, stick to your agreement as much as possible.

The e-mails you send out will reflect your professionalism and attention to details. Watch out for spelling mistakes. Take your time. A thank-you note should remain a thank-you note—short and to the point. Some people prefer e-mail, and very few are still using the old traditional method—that is, a handwritten note. Even in this high-tech world, handwritten is always more personal than e-mail. Nevertheless, it's worth saying that an e-mail gets there faster, so do consider how fast you want your message to be read.

7

Dining Etiquette

INTRODUCTION

It is very important, both professionally and personally, that you master the art of dining etiquette. Your table manners reflect on your corporate culture as well as your etiquette in general.

What do you feel when you dine with a messy or loud eater? What impression does this person leave? Certainly not a good one. If you do not have proper dining etiquette, it is difficult to hide it.

More and more, importance is given to dining etiquette. Business ideas are proposed or concepts are born over business meals. Do not ruin an opportunity because of your lack of table manners.

If your business partner is not showing proper dining etiquette, do not follow his example; stay loyal to your good manners.

GENERAL TABLE ETIQUETTE IN BUSINESS

- Gentlemen should unbutton their jackets upon taking their seats and button up when leaving the table.
- International tradition dictates that the host (gender aside) should instigate the raising of glasses and make a brief toast, signaling his or her fellow diners to drink.
- On official occasions, the guests of honor are served first, followed by the ladies, and finally the gentlemen. If there is no special occasion, the rule of "ladies first" applies.
- All plates are served and cleared from the right.
- Drinks are poured from the right.
- When you have finished eating, you should leave your plate in front of you and not push it away to the middle of the table or to the side.
- Leave your cutlery at four o'clock on your plate to indicate that you are not eating anymore.
- The knife blade should always be inside (facing toward you).
- It is very important to be discreet when conversing. You should talk to your table only.

We discovered a true story in the local newspaper of Geneva that I think is worth mentioning. Three professionals were discussing and complaining about the disadvantages of their profession. The negativity was omnipresent. Names were mentioned and critiques made about different people and nationalities. Little did the trio realize that nearby, a journalist was listening to their conversation. The following day, their whole story was published in the local newspaper, in which the journalist used irony to show how unjustified and selfish their grievances were. The journalist mentioned neither the professionals' names nor their employer, but he did specify the field. The trio had given enough description that they were identified with their story. They were severely warned by their management and became a laughingstock—thus the importance of speaking to your table and not to others.

During your business meals, be careful of the following:

- Avoid addressing someone when they have just taken a mouthful.
- Avoid talking with your mouth full. (It is for a good reason that you were told from a young age to finish your food before speaking.)
- Avoid making noise while eating
- Do not pick your teeth or use a toothpick at the dining table.

- Avoid using your phone during a business meal. In case you are obliged to, warn your dinner companions beforehand and excuse yourself.

- Burping is accepted in certain parts of the world, where it shows that you have eaten well. However, in this globalized world, it is a generally frowned upon. Be careful where you are conducting business and who you want to impress.

- Use your napkin to wipe your mouth but not to clean other parts of your body, especially not to blow your nose or to wipe sweat.

- Avoid laying your personal items on the table; this is a disturbance for not only the other diners but also the server.

- During business, do not sample others' dishes unless you are very well acquainted with them.

- Do not put your napkin on your chair. (Despite what is sometimes promoted, the chair is where you put your posterior, and your napkin is what you use to clean your mouth.)

- If you have to get up, place your napkin to the left or right of your place setting, not in the middle where you plate is supposed to be. If you remain seated, your napkin is placed on your lap. (It is the first thing you do upon taking your seat.)

- Avoid drinking from different spots of your glass. Using the same spot will prevent leaving lipstick smudges or oily food traces all over the rim of your glass.

- Allow your host to order first, so you can follow his lead on the number of courses to take. If your host is not ordering first, ask for his recommendations.
- Do not order the most expensive food on the menu, especially when you are not paying.
- Avoid ordering food that is tricky to eat, such as spare ribs, lobster, or spaghetti.
- Do not rush your guests into their meals; try to match their pacing if possible.
- A business meal is a chance to catch up on business and to impress your loyal clients, certainly not to conduct meetings that need to be recorded and require serious follow-ups. The dining table bears no space for note-taking.
- Be careful when you are eating food with sauce not to spray yourself and the person in front of you.
- Do not hold your cutlery in a fist.
- Do not butter your bread in the air but on the side plate, which should remain on the left side at all times.
- Do not lick your cutlery or fingers.
- If you are on a diet, it is not a good idea to organize or attend a business meal unless you decide to cheat.
- If you are wearing a hat, you should take your hat off when you take your seat.

- Sniffing endlessly is inconsiderate; do excuse your-self and blow your nose.
- The host is the one who pays the bill.
- Know your limits with alcohol.

DRINKING PRACTICES AND CUSTOMS

During your business meal, remember to go easy on the alcohol. You do not want to ruin your reputation or say something daring because you have had one glass too many.

If everyone at the table is ordering wine, do not ask, "What would you like to drink?" Your guests might ask for the Petrus 1979, which might be out of your company's budget. Give them a choice between red or white wine and suggest (with wine knowledge) a good, affordable wine. If you do not have wine knowledge, ask the sommelier for suggestion before your guests arrive. If you are opting for champagne, tell you guest, "May I offer you a glass of champagne?" Always let the guests choose first. Why? Using the above technique will prevent your guests from feeling awkward for taking wine when you are not. They might think they are not allowed to drink or that your budget does not permit it. You need to put your guests at ease.

It is a time-honored tradition that the host raises his glass first—usually making a brief toast or saying a few words of welcome—and gives the signal to drink. At all official occasions and private events of a formal nature, the rules of protocol should be observed. You do not come off well if you start drinking before everyone else, especially if you are the guest.

SEATING PLACEMENTS

If you are the host, your guest of honor should be seated on your right. If the dinner includes just the two of you, ensure that you give your guest the best seat of the two (taking into consideration the view and the walkways).

If you are hosting a couple of people for a meal, do not be the last one to turn up but the first. Give yourself time to organize your seating plan. Depending on the size and type of the event, as well as the number of attendees, name cards can be useful so that your guests can identify their seats. A table plan at the entrance can also be helpful.

If you are a guest, do not shift name cards on the tables because you would prefer to sit next to someone else. It is rude to do so. Do not even think of asking for a change. There might be a good strategic reason that the host has placed you in this particular seat.

YOUR CUTLERY

When you take your seat, do not fidget with your cutlery, as this is a sign of boredom or stress, not a positive sign. If there are many types of cutlery placed in front of you for a set menu, start from the outside cutlery and work your way to the inside. If there is not a set menu, the minimum cutlery will be placed in front of you and, according to what you have ordered, adjusted. The rule of "from outside to the inside" still remains.

As you speak during the meal, place your cutlery on your plate to free up your hands to gesture.

If you are not finished, place your cutlery on your plate, the knife at four o'clock and the fork at eight o'clock, the tips touching on your plate and the handles not resting on the table. When you have finished your course, place both types of cutlery at four o'clock on your plate, a sign that your plate can be cleared.

ORGANIZING A BUSINESS MEAL

If you do not plan your business meal well ahead, you might find that your business meal becomes a hassle or a bore to organize. A business meal planned well ahead of time is more likely to have a positive outcome than a last-minute one.

- Why do you want to organize a business meal?
- What do you want to achieve?
  - o   Is it to thank someone?
  - o   Is it simply to catch up?
- Are you inviting one or more people? If more than one:
  - o   Are they working for the same company?
  - o   Do they know each other?
  - o   Can they stand each other?
- Is it the first time you have invited these people?
- How well do you know these people?
- How important is this meal?

If you are not used to organizing a business meal, ensure you know the answers to these questions. It will give you an objective and a frame to work within. It is very important to know the dietary constraints of your guest(s) in order to choose the location properly. Give your guest(s) two or three selections of restaurants to choose from, or choose a restaurant that has good diversity in its menu as well as a good reputation. This way, you ensure that everyone can find something to his or her liking on the menu.

Impress your guest(s) by proposing restaurants you are familiar with. If a restaurant is new to you, do not hesitate to test it prior to your event. Become familiar with the place and allow the staff to get accustomed to you and your habits; this will ease organization and increase your importance. It will also be easier for you to trust that the staff will follow your guidelines and preferences accordingly.

The restaurant chosen should be well adapted to hold a conversation without any sort of noise disturbance or distraction that could be to the detriment of your business meal. Do not hesitate to call the restaurant to stress the importance of your business meal and your sitting preference if necessary. Reconfirming the business meeting with your guest(s) one or two days prior is also recommended if you originally set the meeting a couple of weeks earlier.

If your invitation was extended over the phone, be sure to send a written confirmation right after, mentioning the name, town, and phone number of the restaurant. If you and your guests are in two different cities, you do not want them to be at the Lake Restaurant in Geneva while you are at the Lake Restaurant in Lausanne, as there are often different restaurants with the same name. If you feel that your guests are not acquainted with the place, give directions and explain parking areas.

We highly recommend that you give guests a time frame during which their presence is needed: for example, "I am free from noon to two o'clock to meet up with you." This will ensure that both parties free up space and don't have to rush through the meal. A friendly reminder at the beginning of the meal will help you find out if the time frame has been altered or if it can be expended, both for you and your guest(s).

At no point is it acceptable to arrive late at a meal, especially one you are hosting. Not only is tardiness rude, but it shows the lack of importance you give to your guest(s). When your guest(s) arrive, you should always stand up to greet with a handshake.

If your host has not arrived when you get to a restaurant, wait for him or her in the lobby or waiting area if possible.

If some of your guests are late, inform the restaurant staff, who will direct them to your table.

PAYING THE BILL

When the bill arrives at the table, there is often an awkward moment where everyone wonders who is taking care of it. Often there is a jovial argument as all try to pay the bill.

Regardless of gender, the host is the one taking care of the bill. At no point should the guest be paying or sharing the bill. The bill should be paid away from the table. When you choose the restaurant, you can tell and remind the staff that the bill should be put on your company's tab. If this method is not possible, you can excuse yourself to go and pay away from the eyes of your invitees. It will take a few minutes to do so.

Recently, my husband and I were invited to a dinner hosted by one of his business partners. Four of my husband's colleagues were present, along with their spouses. Everything went smoothly, and when it was time to leave, two of the wives asked about the bill. Ignorant of the above-mentioned code, they did not realize that Fred, the business partner, had taken care of the bill in a very discreet manner.

THANK-YOU NOTES

To come to a business meal, all people present have taken time out of their personal or business schedules to meet up. The host has taken time to ensure a smooth and enjoyable encounter. No matter the outcome of the meal, a thank-you note will always be appreciated.

The note's purpose is to express one's gratitude for the meal and the time spent in each other's company. It can also be a way to recap decisions made during the meal. A sincere thank-you note should not come only from the guest but also from the host. This action can brighten the receiver's day as well as portray a professional image of yourself.

Your thank-you can be sent in the form of an e-mail, phone call, or even SMS if you have established that the receiver prefers this form of communication.

Just because you have been invited for a meal, this does not mean that you are obliged to invite the person back in the near future. Extend an invitation because you have the answers to the questions noted in the "Organizing a Business Meal" section.

8

Technology Etiquette

INTRODUCTION

Each time you open a package to discover your new smartphone (or tablet), you discover its physical aspects as well as its utility. So far, little has been taught about how you should make use of your smartphone in a respectful manner. Some people become automatically conscious of their surroundings while using their new tools and are careful to prevent noise and other disturbances.

How many times have you attended a concert, the cinema, or your children's show—when up goes a screen trying to get a picture or video? What is inconsiderate at this precise moment is the impact that person and his or her smartphone have on those sitting nearby.

I was at my children's school Christmas show, an emotional moment for me, seeing my sons (who hate singing) on the stage singing. The show started. Less than a minute later, a tablet came up, and I could not see my sons through the entire concert unless I tilted my head back and forth.

With technology and its continuous development comes responsibilities and awareness. The presence of the new electronic devices is not only what you should be careful of, but the way you make use of them.

Good manners and respect for others will make you question whether your act is disrupting or offending anyone.

For example, say you're in a very nice quiet restaurant, and there goes a ringing tone. You may think that it was an accident; after all, we all forget to silence our phones sometimes. But then the person converses loudly for the whole room to hear. Is that good manners? Is it respectful toward the others in the room?

For another example, you are conducting business, and your business partner cannot stop fidgeting with his device. Are you sure he is listening to you? How do you feel about it?

E-MAIL ETIQUETTE

E-mail has made communication much faster globally. It is considered to be among the most widely used forms of communication.

In early years, communication was done via smoke signals, then carrier pigeons, horseback delivery, and boat delivery. Back then, messages took time to reach their destinations. Telegraphs and airplanes revolutionized written communication thanks to their rapidity.

The telephone made verbal communication global. However, it remained a luxury for many years. Not everyone could afford one. Over time, having a phone became a must. It was hard to conceive that a house did not possess a telephone. Years later, the telephone shared the market with the fax machine. The fax machine facilitated the exchange of written communication locally and internationally.

Internet and e-mail appeared, and communication became global and instant. Within seconds, a written message travels from one continent to the other.

While it is now very easy to send a proper message quickly wherever you are, messages are being sent with more and more errors—and less and less consideration for others.

Here are some rules to follow when communicating through e-mail:

- Do not write your message without a subject.
- Do not write your whole message in the subject section.
- Do not write your message in capitals, as this comes across as aggressive.
- Do not mark your message as URGENT if it is not, as no one will take you seriously when it is really urgent.
- Avoid copying unnecessary people in your message.
- Avoid using "reply to all" if not needed.
- Avoid sending a lot of e-mails when you can send one.
- Conclude your e-mail with a closing line along with your signature.
- If you accidentally overlook an e-mail, excuse yourself instead of trying to prove you did not receive it. Never forget that the sender has a trace.
- If the topic seems complicated to write down, discuss it over the phone and summarize or reconfirm via e-mail at a later stage. Your conversation will help you find the right words to put in an e-mail.
- Watch out for spelling and grammar mistakes. One letter *N* too many can change the whole meaning

of the word or sentence. A little word can turn a positive message into a negative one.

- Avoid sending long e-mails; get to the point. If your e-mails are too long, chances are that they won't be read or understood fully, as the reader might get distracted. Those e-mails may then be marked as "read" without any action being taken.

PHONE ETIQUETTE

Representing yourself or your company over the phone is as important as presenting yourself in person. Very often a telephone conversation can be the trigger to a potential collaboration.

It is therefore crucial to be courteous, professional, and respectful. Your smile should not be reserved only for when you are having face-to-face interaction. When you are talking over the phone, the other person can hear in your voice if you are smiling or not.

As you are not being seen, only verbal communication is being used. Thus, when you are on a business call, do not let yourself get distracted, as this can cause a bad information exchange.

When you are calling someone, greet the person and introduce yourself. If applicable, introduce the company you are presenting as well, before requesting to talk to the desired person. Ensure that your phone call is not done at peak call times or unwelcome periods for the receiver and that you have enough time to calmly make the call. Do consider time differences as well as lunch and closure times.

Speak clearly and softly. Talking on the phone is not the same as talking in person; many types of interference can affect a conversation. Ensure that the person you're calling understands what you consider important by repeating if necessary.

Before answering or calling someone, ensure that you are in a good position to talk, with good network availability and minimum noise disturbance. Do not answer or call for business when you are eating or drinking.

Talking over the phone with a stranger is not everybody's favorite thing. Sometimes language barriers as well as cultural differences might make pronunciation complicated. Some names can be surprising, depending of the culture.

Philippe has been conducting business internationally for several years. Before he started a conversation with a new associate, once the introductions had been made, he repeated the associate's name to confirm that he had the pronunciation right. Philippe asked the other person to correct him if he was wrong.

Although some companies allow cell phone usage at work, you should not let it become a disturbance for others. Watch out for your ringtone. If you are in public spaces, it is considerate to put your cell phone on vibrate mode. A novelty ringtone can be funny when you first hear it, but it can look unprofessional in a work environment.

Holding a private phone conversation in front of your colleagues is not very professional. You need to find a quiet space to avoid disrupting others. If you receive a non-urgent private phone call, the best solution is to postpone the call to a later time.

If you are attending a meeting, unless you have excused yourself or warned your fellow attendees that you are expecting an important phone call or message, there is no reason for you to be playing with your phone, as it is rude to do so. Your phone should be on silent or in your office, away from others' eyes.

Text messages are very common and acceptable by some as a form of business communication. If you tend to send text messages for business, ensure that this method is accepted and preferred by the person at the receiving end. If it is, avoid using acronyms, as these are not always understood by all, depending on culture, age, and professional background.

To stay connected despite the continents that separate us, my little sister and I use written forms of communication, either e-mail or SMS. It has become easier to stay in touch, but it is complicated at times to understand my sister's messages, as she has a habit of using acronyms. Very often, it takes more than one message to understand the essence of the sentence, when one would have sufficed if done properly.

As a final note on this topic, remember to not keep your phone in your pocket. It will make your pocket appear bulky and ruin the cut of your clothes.

SOCIAL MEDIA ETIQUETTE

Social media facilitates people's abilities to stay in touch and share information. In certain cases, social media helps information reach you faster. Social media is also used for entertainment or leisure, but it plays a vital role in the business world. It facilitates networking and is used as a marketing and selling tool.

Depending on the way it is used, social media can enhance your professional life, or it can ruin your career and business.

We decided to research the role of social media in a recruitment process.

Human-resources managers who participated in our research stated that, even if it was not ethically correct, their curiosity got them to look up certain candidates online when they sent in their applications. Unfortunately or fortunately for the candidates, the HR managers get an idea of each applicant based on what they find on social media.

It is not only what you say on social media that is of importance but also how often you are connected. Social media should be used with respect for others but most importantly with respect for yourself.

Even if you think what you put online is private, accessible only to your circle of friends or followers, just remember that your friends and followers have other friends and followers, and their friends and followers have other friends and followers. So be careful—do not ruin your chance of success in life because of a moment of fun posted on social media.

Here are some rules to follow when using social media:

- When posting pictures or videos, avoid nudity.
- Avoid any photo portraying you in an awkward situation: drunk, drinking, fighting, or in bad company.
- Be aware of your privacy settings; don't let everyone access your data and postings.
- Know your audience.
- Depending of your job, be careful when expressing your opinion about sensitive subjects like politics, sexual orientation, religion, or money.
- Do not post any messages about your work or colleagues, especially if it's negative or confidential.
- Be careful when socializing with your clients.

VIDEO ETIQUETTE

Conducting a business meeting or interview via video conference is a common practice. Using video instead of a regular phone call brings people closer.

Compared to a phone call, a video conference is not only cheaper, but it also guarantees both parties' undivided attention.

Before launching a video conference, guarantee that your equipment is operational and does not suffer from disturbances or technical issues. Testing your equipment first will help prevent bad surprises during your video conference.

A video conference needs to be conducted in a quiet area away from distractions. Avoid conducting a video conference in a public area, as noise interference and visual movement can be very disruptive. Never forget that the person on the other side will not only see your face but also what is around you; therefore, it's always preferable to choose a place without visual disruptions. If your next-year strategy is written on a board behind you, you would not want your client to be reading it instead of listening to you.

9

Social Etiquette

Unlike business etiquette, where importance is given to hierarchy and power, social etiquette gives importance to gender, age, or weakness. Very often, people tend to mix the two etiquettes' rules.

Depending on the situation you are faced with, the rule of good manners remains. However, the person you give importance to will differ between a business and a social environment.

If you go to a business meal with Peter, your CEO, and Mary, your operations manager, Peter is the one you will need to flatter. You will not be obliged to pull out Mary's chair, as this meal is being held in a business environment.

However, if you are going a private meal with Peter and Mary, social etiquette and manners request that the door is opened for Mary and that her chair is pulled. She is the one who gets the best seat.

If you follow good manners, have consideration and empathy for others, and are humble, it will be difficult to behave incorrectly.

Social etiquette can differ from one country to the other. Through observation, you can learn to behave correctly in different situations. The way you dress, communicate, and dine will differ from Europe to Asia and Asia to Africa. When you are discovering a new culture, step in slowly—watch, listen, learn, and ask questions. Do not assume that the rules are the same in this new culture or that your culture does it better. Make your own opinions, and don't follow stereotypes, as these may affect your judgement and reactions.

During his first business trip to Egypt, Pascal was invited to a wedding by his longtime business partner. As comfortable as he felt conducting business with his Egyptian associate, he was totally lost when it came to this private event. Instead of adopting the French way of behaving (the ways of his home country), Pascal asked how he was expected to be dress, what gift was acceptable, and what would be expected of him during the wedding, to avoid any faux pas. The differences were big, and he was happy that he had asked.

You will not make a fool of yourself by asking, but you will make a fool of yourself if you make assumptions and get it wrong.

MIND YOUR LANGUAGE

With globalization, people are traveling and conducting business away from home more and more, sometimes away from a known culture. If your business is global, you will often conduct business in a language other than your native one.

Customers and business associates very much appreciate hearing someone making the effort to speak their language, especially when that person is in their country.

It is, however, very important to master a language properly before using it for business to avoid offending others by using a word incorrectly or by accidentally saying something obscene.

In one of my business meetings, I said a word that was not very "businessy" and that made the crowd laugh. I was embarrassed when I realized my error. I have since learned to never use this word again during my business meetings.

Depending where people are from and what encounters they have in their lives, they get used to a certain way of saying things. If you are not careful, your intonation and word choices can be offensive, or they can be considered slang or overly familiar. Thus, they would be not very flattering.

Refrain from using slang or overly familiar words in business meetings, especially when you are new to a position or partner. Make a good habit by using the right vocabulary from the beginning.

Watch the terms and vocabulary you use when conversing; these can say a lot about you and your background. You do not want to lose a deal because of your word choice and intonation.

Conclusion

Thanks to the exchanges and seminars we have delivered over the years, we, the Business Etiquette Associates have managed to share our knowledge and experiences with many people across the world.

We hope that through this book we have managed to give you tools that will help you lead your professional life with more confidence.

We believe that the book will give you the basics, but nothing will replace practice, practice, practice. Remember that, as they say, practice makes perfect.

Make your own experiences, and be successful.

Acknowledgments

Audrey

Christelle and Laurent, without you, I might not have discovered this path.

Olivier, my dear husband, you took care of this edition and shared your good and bad business experiences. Your expectations and business ethics made it easy to write this book. Without you, the book might have stayed in the closet.

Luka and Arno, your patience, pride, and encouragement made this project possible. Thanks to you, your mummy discovered that there is absolutely no wrong age to start learning about business etiquette.

Annabelle, through the years, your experience and your wisdom have brought so much. Thank you.

Annabelle

Praline, many thanks for the experience you shared with me at the beginning of my career.

Antoinette and Joanna, you helped me in many ways, I could count on your open-minded advice

Llano, you were so patient in encouraging me to go ahead and write the present book.

The day I met Audrey, I knew we could write a book about modern business etiquette. Shortly after we started working together, I suggested we put down our experience. Thanks to our documentation and writings Audrey started to put things together in order to write the present book in English.

Audrey, thank you for the time and knowledge you invested in our present work, and thanks also to Olivier, your dear husband, for his involvement.

Audrey & Annabelle

All those who shared their experiences, asked their questions, and trusted us, thank you. We hope this book will enhance your business lives.

All those whose names have been mentioned in the real-life stories of this book, you know who you are, and we thank you for your inspirations.

About the Authors

Annabelle Utelli, originally from Switzerland, is the co-founder of Business Etiquette Consultants. She is an expert in non-verbal communication, modern business etiquette and body language since many years.

Annabelle followed international training on Image, Fashion, Communication and has since then been working as a Personal and Professional Image and Communication Consultant.

Her previous professional background brought her to work in international firms of luxurious standards, such as watches, jewelry and the fashion industry.

With a very solid background and enriching experience, Annabelle Utelli shares her passion to what human being considers very important; Self-Image, body language, behavior, verbal and non-verbal communication.

Annabelle has already published her first book on Manner for Children in 2010.

Audrey Bonvin Dechoux, originally from Seychelles, is the cofounder of Business Etiquette Consultants. She has been coaching business etiquette in different countries since 2011.

Audrey obtained a dual degree in hospitality management and business management from Northwood University in Switzerland. Audrey also followed a three-year course on body language in Switzerland.

She has worked in luxury hotels, travel agencies, and several hospitality institutions dedicated to education in Seychelles and Switzerland.

Audrey is currently following her studies to acquire more knowledge and experience.

Audrey lives in Montreux, Switzerland, with her two sons and her husband.